CW00519567

UNDER
THE
DUVET
OF
DARKNESS

Edited by Boiledbeetle

UNDER THE DUVET OF DARKNESS

Poems written by angry women for angry women

because

WOMEN WON'T WHEESHT

Edited by Boiledbeetle

© This collection: Boiledbeetle 2023

All rights reserved

ISBN: 9798388092182

No part of this publication may be reproduced, distributed, or transmitted in any form or by any means, including photocopying, recording, or other electronic or mechanical methods, without the prior written permission of the copyright owner, except as permitted by UK copyright law.

March 2023

CONTENTS

CHAPTER ELEVEN: SOCK PUPPETRY

CHAPTER TWELVE: THE MULTI-VERSE 91

CHAPTER THIRTEEN: TEA BREAK 101

FOREWORD

In honour of Magdalen Berns, who co-founded the Scottish campaign group For Women Scotland, 100% of the profit from the sale of this book* will be donated to For Women Scotland.

For Women Scotland are a group of women from all over Scotland. They work to protect and strengthen women and children's rights.

The group was founded in June 2018 due to unease about women's rights, and how they would be affected by the Scottish Government's plans to reform the Gender Recognition Act 2004 to allow for self-ID of sex.

For Women Scotland** do not receive any public money and are not aligned to any political party. All the staff are volunteers.

**"It's not hate to defend your rights,
and it's not hate to speak the truth."**

Magdalen Berns

(1983 – 2019)

*Please note that whilst the profit will be donated to For Women Scotland they are not involved, nor are they responsible in any way for the themes, contents or publication of this book.

**For Women Scotland has been registered as a not-for-profit company since July 2020 (Company number: SC669393). More information about For Women Scotland can be found at: https://forwomen.scot/

COPYRIGHT ACKNOWLEDGEMENTS

POEM COPYRIGHT HOLDERS

© ArabellaScott: Poem 68
© ArcaneWireless: Poems 6, 40, 41, 78
© Babdoc: Poem 21
© beastlyslumber: Poems 8, 31, 32, 57
© BethDuttonsTwin: Poem 16
© Boiledbeetle: Poems 2, 3, 14, 24, 26, 27, 34, 36, 37, 39, 42, 44, 49, 51, 53, 58, 60, 61, 62, 63, 65, 66, 67, 70, 71, 74, 80
© BoiledsCatOverlord: Poem 61
© ClitoralViolence: Poems 35, 56, 61
© CuriousEats: Poem 61
© DialSquare: Poem 19
© Elainesfakemingemerkin: Poem 28
© FlirtsWithRhinos: Poems 20, 23, 54
© NicolasMerkinNemesis: Poem 64
© NoFlowersForEmily: Poem 4
© Oher: Poem 9
© RaininginDarling: Poem 10
© RealFeminist: Poems 11, 13, 15
© Ritasueandbobtoo9: Poems 12, 17, 25, 29, 33, 43, 48, 69, 76, 77
© Sazzasez: Poems 7, 75
© TerfranosaurusVagina: Poems 1, 30, 35, 46, 47, 52, 59, 61
© TheBiologyStupid: Poems 72, 73
© UsernameWithheld: Poem 79
© Waitwhat23: Poems 5, 18, 22, 50, 55, 61
© WeAreSarah: Poem 45
© WomenofExtremes: Poem 38

COMMENT COPYRIGHT HOLDERS

© ArabellaScott
© Boiledbeetle
© CuriousEats
© Dodecaheidyin
© FlirtsWithRhinos
© Ramblingnamechanger
© RealFeminist
© Ritasueandbobtoo9
© TightFistedWozerk
© Waitwhat23

ACKNOWLEDGEMENTS

The users of the FWR (Feminism and Women's Rights) board on Mumsnet are continually appreciative, despite the numerous times posts get deleted, that MNHQ gives us the platform to talk about women's rights.

On the FWR board we have the freedom to centre our thoughts on just women and children. We usually discuss the effects that the current push of gender ideology is having on women and children. But we also talk about food. A lot. Mainly cheese currently.

The poems in this book were posted under 25 different usernames. We are grateful to the other posters that read our poems and especially those that commented and helped bump our witterings back up the list of threads.

On a personal note, thank you to TerfranosaurusVagina for posting the poem that set us all off. Thanks also to ArabellaScott, Ramblingnamechanger and Sazzasez for their much appreciated help whilst preparing this book.

I'm sending a huge virtual hug to BH for telling me to, and I paraphrase, stop procrastinating and do something useful with my poems.

We can all be grateful to my sister who, if you are actually reading this, will have put up with a meltdown from me whilst trying to publish it!

Lastly, and most importantly, thank you to all the poem writers, and comment writers, who gave me permission to use their words in this book. I am eternally grateful.

Boiledbeetle x

INTRODUCTION

Please can these be collated, maybe sold for campaigning funds?

Comment by Ramblingnamechanger

I'm sorely tempted to write to Poetry Please on Radio 4 and ask them to do an extended special for Hogmanay just about this thread.

Comment by Dodecaheidyin

To the women of Scotland,

On 22nd December 2022 with the passing of The Gender Recognition Reform (Scotland) Bill a lot of women all over the UK, very rightly, became very angry.

On 28th December 2022 at 1.04am on a forum somewhere in the depths of the internet a thread was started.

The OP, TerfranosaurusVagina, having mulled on her annoyance and anger at Nicola Sturgeon, First Minister of Scotland, decided to put her emotions to good use and posted a poem, her 'Ode to Nicola'.

This book is a collection of 80 of the poems from many posters who followed the OP's example. Angry women from all over channelled their annoyance at not just Nicola but at the whole of this 'Brave New World' parallel universe we currently find ourselves living in.

Now that was going to be it, a nice short introduction. Then, on 16th January 2023, Westminster stepped in to issue an order under Section 35 of The Scotland Act 1998. This prevents the GRR (Scotland) Bill from proceeding to Royal Assent.

In response Nicola Sturgeon stated her government was likely to mount a legal challenge. This would be through a judicial review, in order to assess the lawfulness of the Scottish Secretary's decision. At the time of publication (March 2023) we are still waiting to see what will happen.

Then, in what was the most fortuitous of timing, things went even more to shit for dear Nicola.

On 24th January 2023, at the High Court of Justiciary in Glasgow, a man called Adam Graham, claiming to be a transwoman named Isla Bryson, was convicted of raping two women and initially sent to Cornton Vale, a women's prison in Scotland. A photograph of Adam Graham/Isla Bryson outside the court wearing a rather fetching outfit of blond wig, full make up, manicured fingernails, and a very tight pair of pink leggings that highlighted the very thing he'd raped two women with, was seen around the world.

At this point more of the general public began to take notice and were beginning to realise what had been happening, quietly in the background, whilst women were shut down and called bigots and TERFs for trying to point out the problems with self-ID.

Even the eventual decision to send Adam Graham/Isla Bryson to a male prison caused more headaches for Nicola Sturgeon. It was a surprise to a lot of people to discover that according to the First Minister of Scotland we now have three sexes: man, woman and rapist.

On 15th February 2023, at an unexpected news conference, Nicola Sturgeon announced her intention to resign as First Minister of Scotland with the words "In my head and my heart, I know that time is now."

Bye Nicola!

So, back to the poems... As you read this you are hopefully sat at home, feet up with your favourite drink and snack at hand. We're hoping you're not stuck hunkered down for hours in a building, waiting for the insult throwing, pie throwing, liquid throwing and, sometimes, fist throwing thugs to go home for their tea.

But wherever you may be right now we hope the following poems help the time pass a little more pleasantly.

Your anger is our anger.

Women Won't Wheesht.

Women of the Mumsnet FWR board March 2023

CHAPTER ONE:

NICOLA

Who knew! Nicola, a muse to women's poetry.

Comment by Boiledbeetle

Sturgeon is a hard one. Nic on the other hand...

Comment by FlirtsWithRhinos

POEM 1 TerfranosaurusVagina 28th December 2022 1.04am

ODE TO NICOLA

Feminist to your fingertips
So many lies are passing your lips
Trans activist to your toenails
Innumerable safeguard fails
Misogynist to your merkin
Policies are tear jerkin'
Destroyer of women's rights
You're so superior, yet shite

But most of all... you're a hypocrite.

POEM 2 Boiledbeetle 28th December 2022 1.33am

NICOLA - OF THE STURGEON KIND ONLY

Narcissistic

Idiotic

Crowing

Odious

Lying

Arsewipe

POEM 3 Boiledbeetle 28th December 2022 2.32am

QUESTIONS FROM THE AUDIENCE

Do you think about us now?
Did you consider us before?
Will you remember on your death bed?
Will our faces come to the fore?

The good you could have done.
The legacy to be left.
You could have helped your country.
Instead of leaving half of us bereft.

We think about US now.
We considered ALL before.
But I guess we didn't swing our dicks enough.
And now will suffer evermore.

You betrayed us.
You abandoned us.
You put you up front and centre.
The amazing Nicola, the great experimenter.

You're the leader of a country.
And you just pushed half under a bus.
You're a disgrace to your country.
And I hope it haunts you to the end, as it will for all of us.

POEM 4 NoFlowersForEmily 28th December 2022 3.53am

YOU terrible
TERRIBLE
PEOPLE.

IF ONLY
ANY of them
GAVE A SINGLE FUCK
about women,
or our daughters.

GOD KNOWS
how she sleeps at night.
And the rest of them.

SEE YOU IN HELL NICOLA.

POEM 5 Waitwhat23 28th December 2022 9.57am

TO NICOLA - A SERIES OF HAIKUS

The future was bright,
Until you betrayed women.
We won't forget this.

Girls want to be boys,
Ever increasing numbers.
No problem at all?

Spaces for women,
Are taken away for men.
A big shrug from you.

A woman's clothes, hair,
Doesn't make her a woman.
We're not a costume.

We're really angry,
Us adult human females.
We won't forget this.

RealFeminist 28th December 2022 11.11am

DISNAE RHYME PROPERLY.

POEM 6 ArcaneWireless 28th December 2022 12.50pm

(Inspired by Ballad of Barry & Freda (Let's Do It) by Victoria Wood)

I can't do it. I can't do it.
We've surely had about enough.
No places are safe spaces.
The woman
Speaks a lot of guff.
Fucks flying.
She's trying,
Hard to convince us all she wasn't christened Brian.
I can't do it. I won't do it tonight.

I can't do it. I can't do it.
The woman surely went too far.
Rights flying, they're dying.
I'm gonna have to burn my bra.
She's mastered,
Being a bastard.
The only excuse for this is that she's bloody plastered.
I can't do it. I can't do it tonight.

POEM 7 Sazzasez 28th December 2022 1.03pm

(Inspired by Lydia the Tattooed Lady by Yip Harburg and Harold Arlen)

Nicola, oh Nicola.
Say have you met Nicola?
Nicola the Men's Rights Lady?

She has no time for rape survivors,
Power and pandering are her drivers.

Nicola oh Nicola, few could be trickier.
Oh Nicola the Queen of DARVO.
At her back is the money of Pharma shills,
And selling out women's rights sure pays the bills.
And proudly above it the saltire flag thrills,
Painted pink and blue for Nicola.

POEM 8 beastlyslumber 28th December 2022 1.12pm

What do you get when you vote for Nicola?
You get a lot of pain, hurt and sorrow,
And men in your rape refuge tomorrow.
I'll never vote for her again.
She'll never lead Scotland again.

What do you get when you throw out laws,
Meant to keep women and children safe?
You get a lot of violence, trauma and rape.
We'll never vote her in again.
History will put her in the rubbish bin.

POEM 9 Oher 28th December 2022 2.18pm

There was once a blond man in London
Who thought ruling would be some fun
So he lied and bullied and cajoled
'Till out of a Union Britain rolled
So he could seize the crown
And turn his frown upside down
Unfortunately this bodged the country
Nurses and teachers now need meals for free
No one can even afford energy
But Boris has great tales to tell over tea
Nicola had watched the whole thing
And liked the look of everything
"This is genius" thought she
"Divide the country
Then everyone will vote for me!
But, how best to create more unrest?
How to divide the electorate into two,
And confuse till they don't know what is true?"
Nicola mused and Nicola planned
She decided the country must be unmanned
The country that gave kilts to the world
Must now claim a skirt = you're a girl
Let men wander where they will
Rapists in women's prisons? Sure why not
As long as Nicola gets her plot
"A vote for me is a vote for the free"
Nicola yells
"And you're a witch if you disagree!
Who probably smells."
Someone said something about free speech
So Nicola made sure that was out of reach
"No vote can possibly be free
Everyone must vote for me
Stop the kids learning history
And everyone tell:
Authoritarianism always ends well."

POEM 10 RaininginDarling 28th December 2022 4.21pm

There once was a woman in Scotland,
Who pushed through a bill, a real botched one.
"Feminist to her tips."
Said the lies on her lips.
So Elaine flashed her (faux) front bottom.

POEM 11 RealFeminist 28th December 2022 4.50pm

RIGHT YOUS ARE ALL FOR IT
AHM CALLIN THE POLIS

YE CANNAE JUST HATE CRIME AT WILL.

I ADVISE YE NO RISK IT
IT'S TAKIN THE BISCUIT

TAE WAX ON WI OOT CHECKIN OER

LADYRAP THAT'S NO SCRIPTIT
THAT'S SWEARY AND PISS RIPPED

AND HUSNAE BEEN CLEARED BY A MAN.

QUIT WI THE WRONGTHINK
IF YE DINNAE WANT FRISKIN

BY A BOABBY WI UNCERTAIN PRONOUNS.

POEM 12 Ritasueandbobtoo9 28th December 2022 10.35pm

Nicola with all her ken,
bent over backwards for the men.
It's quite safe so she said,
now women's rights are totally dead
in the water, in the school,
men in women's prisons,
that's the rule.
Free to stare and intimidate.
No women safe in Scotland's state.

POEM 13 RealFeminist 28th December 2022 11.15pm

READ MA LIPS
I LIE TAE MAH FINGERTIPS.

NEVER MIND SHAKIRA'S HIPS
IF IT TAKS A THREE LINE WHIP

AH'LL TELL YE WHIT A WOMAN IS:

IT'S A FEELIN; A MAN'S WILL
A NAME ON A GAS BILL.

IT'S LIPSTICK AND SHORT SKIRTS
AND WEE DOTTY LOVE HEARTS.

IT'S WHATEVER HE SAYS IT IS.

POEM 14 Boiledbeetle 29th December 2022 11.17am

LISTEN TO ME

Nicola... NICOLA!

Oh, WHAT HAVE YOU DONE?

You've SACRIFICED DAUGHTERS

In favour of son?

You've OPENED UP WOMANHOOD

TO all of the MEN!

YOU'RE A TRAITOR TO WOMEN

Which you bloody well ken!

POEM 15 RealFeminist 29th December 2022 11.46am

NO AHVE NO.

AHVE ALIGNED WI BEST PRACTICE
IN MALTA, WHEREVER THAT IS

AND RELEASED THE LADYPEEN
FAE THE PRISON O THE UNSEEN

INTAE GLIMMERIN SUNLIGHT
AND STRAIGHT ONTAE NEWSNIGHT.

POEM 16 BethDuttonsTwin 29th December 2022 1.22pm

I'm quite laid back
around political discussion.
Generally.

But Nicola...
There's something...
really...
sinister
about her.

Something going on.
Behind the scenes.

No idea what.

But the hardness.
Clear desperation.
Single mindedness.

And, most importantly:

The ignoring of the electorate,
with regards to this issue.
And it's dangers.

Indicates to me there's more to this.

Frightening.

POEM 17 Ritasueandbobtoo9 29th December 2022 10.24pm

Queen Nicola did bow,
to those who knew how,
to manipulate and stipulate,
until they reached checkmate.
By stealth they reached their goal,
but it is women that take the toll.

POEM 18 Waitwhat23 29th December 2022 10.54pm

Numpties like Chapman saying "Sex isn't binary."
Doesn't it give you a wee bit of clarity,
That you've hitched your cart to a horse of insanity.
Because 'The Feral Potato' despises wims,
And yet you dance to all of his whims,
Betraying the women who all chapped and clapped for you,
You say "No, not valid" and cede all our spaces to
The men who hate us and wear women costume.
You're dancing away to their unpleasant tune.
Sense will return at some time but yet,
We'll never forgive and we'll never forget.

POEM 19 DialSquare 30th December 2022 4.16pm

There once was a woman from Irvine,
Who was put in her place by a merkin.
She sold out her sex,
And expected respect,
But most of us think she is barking.

NICOLA

POEM 20 FlirtsWithRhinos 30th December 2022 5.30pm

A fervent First Minister from Irvine
Said "We all know some men are disturbin'.
But that doesn't mean
That a lass wi' a peen
Is the same as a bloke bent on pervin'."

The women of Scotland said "Nic,
You've got the wrong end of the stick.
We don't think transgend girls
Are only pretend girls,
We just need some space without dick."

CHAPTER TWO:

STURGEON

Ooh, Sturgeon is a difficult one!

Comment by Waitwhat23

POEM 21 Babdoc 28th December 2022 9.51am

A fuckwit called Sturgeon
Needed no urgin'
To please men in tights
She trashed women's rights
In hopes that her ratings would surge on.

All hail to we SNP
We are too thick to see
That throwing women under the bus
Does not gain votes
Even from the scrotes
Who usually applaud us.

POEM 22 Waitwhat23 30th December 2022 5.02pm

Sturgeon,
You allow false 'reality' to burgeon.
You really should be learnin'
That you're not a clever person,
And your name will be sung as a dirge(on).

POEM 23 FlirtsWithRhinos 30th December 2022 9.20pm

A treacherous woman called Sturgeon
Decreed sex and gender were mergin'.
So females now face
Trans males in their space,
Instead of them having a third 'un.

CHAPTER THREE:

2023

2024 Happy new year!

Comment by Ritasueandbobtoo9

Happy 2022

Comment by Ritasueandbobtoo9

2023: Paused in right place

Comment by Ritasueandbobtoo9

POEM 24 Boiledbeetle 31st December 2022 11.35pm

I'm slightly early with this but...

2023

Same as... Nope, I'm not having it. We are not starting a new year in a defeatist mood. Let's try again.

2023

Better than 2022 because many many, oh hell Nicola, what have you unleashed?

Many more women have absolutely merkinly (over a million views, won a Terfie, although I'm not sure if it went to Elaine or the merkin) decided that

WOMEN WON'T WHEESHT.

POEM 25 Ritasueandbobtoo9 1st January 2023 2.46pm

2023

Happy 2023.
Nicola, I say to ye
please stop talking shite,
supporting pervs in plain sight.
Make your new year resolution be
to protect women like you and me.

CHAPTER FOUR:

MERKIN

Could be a while for the next verse as got to the third line and laughed. Sigh. Must go do the merkin lady's pelvic exercises.

Comment by Boiledbeetle

POEM 26 Boiledbeetle 28ᵗʰ December 2022 11.52am

I was messing around on ChatGPT and I tried to get it to write a merkin poem but it refused to, because it was a naughty word. So I asked it to write one on wigs, which it happily produced. Now obviously I've had to do some major editorial changes and rewrites, but here's the Artificial Intelligence poem of merkins.

ELAINE AND HER MERKIN

A merkin

A coat of many hues
A symbol of change

A symbol of woman

A way to fight
A way to choose

A tool for self-expression

It highlights the plight
It focuses the woman

It tells a story

It sets the mood
It finds its place

In history

In art
In culture

It can be long
It can be short
It can be straight

ELAINE AND HER MERKIN Cont.

It can be curled
It can be wild
It can be fun

It can be Parliament

It changes with the seasons
With the trends

It follows the beat
It leads the way

It speaks to the soul

It helps us find ourselves
Every single day

So here's to the merkin
In all its glory and hue

May it bring joy
May it bring fun
May it be a source of inspiration

And may it bring justice
For all who wear it.

Women Won't Wheesht

POEM 27 Boiledbeetle 30th December 2022 11.52am

THAT WOMAN IS A CUNT!!

Every time I hear her voice
I clench.

Every time I read her words
I clench.

Every time I check her Twitter
I clench.

Every time I see her face
I clench.

Every time the pee escapes
I picture her in Parliament,

Wearing her Sunday best merkin
And I smile.

And I clench.

Inspiration for poetry comes in the strangest of places, like whilst sticking my head upside down to rinse the shampoo out and at that angle there's not much to look at. God, thought I, Nicola is a fucking cunt, what she did in Parliament...Grr.

Regarding the above poem I should clarify I was thinking of Nicola and it led me to a poem about Elaine. I mean it also works for Nicola if you imagine her lifting her skirt on the floor of the Parliament to reveal a little smiley face merkin. The one with a winky face.

So yeah works both ways, but I was thinking of the wonderful merkin wearer of tales that will be told for years to come to children sat on grannies' knees. So stick that in your pipe and smoke it Nicola.

POEM 28 Elainesfakemingemerkin 31st December 2022 6.45am

A TERFIE ACCEPTANCE SPEECH

Over a million people have seen my minge,
And no, I don't mean the one from the Fringe.
The Parliament stunt got worldwide attention,
Of the very thing that we should not mention.
So by lifting my skirt and shouting out loud,
I've made my family and friend's so very proud.

In response to a tweet from @fem_mb declaring Elaine the winner
of "Protest of the Year – Elaine Miller flashes a merkin at Scottish
Parliament to protest the passing of Self-ID".

@GussieGrips tweeted:

I won a Terfie! Thanks @fem_mb and to the voters. I gather over a
million people have seen my minge. My family are so proud. Arf.
#womenWontWheesht

POEM 29 Ritasueandbobtoo9 2nd January 2023 4.25pm

MERKIN

A merkin used to cover rot,
Now shocked those in power.
Although they don't give a jot,
About a girl in a shower,
Who feels uneasy next to a man,
Who is there because he can.

CHAPTER FIVE:

MRA
TRA
TRANS
PRONOUNS

I don't just sling shit. Think you're thinking of someone else.

Comment by RedAndBlueStripedGolfingUmbrella[1]

POEM 30 TerfranosaurusVagina 28th December 2022 12.26pm

@RedAndBlueStripedGolfingUmbrella
Are you a lady or are you a fella?
Either way it don't really matter
Though if you're going to add to the chatter
Put some thought in before just plopping;
"Be kind, be kind" handmaidens stropping
Gets quite boring after an hour
In fact it's lost all of its power
Hoarding dinosaurs have awoken
And if you don't like what's being spoken
May I suggest you have a think
This is not just blue should be pink
Laydee dicks in female spaces
Are corrupt! These are quiet places
There's no witnesses to disorder
To prevent rape, assault and murder
This will never happen, you tell us
There's no harm in welcoming phallus
From shelters to even just swimming
Include men and you're excluding women.

POEM 31 beastlyslumber 28th December 2022 1.15pm

MRA, it's easy because they say
A man is a woman now, so all bow down
It's okay for MRAs.

123, your safeguards are so easy
To throw in the bin, it's not a sin
123 cos we're all 'women'.

POEM 32 beastlyslumber 28th December 2022 7.58pm

(Inspired by When I Grow Old, I Shall Wear Purple by Jenny Joseph)

When I am a transwoman I shall not wear purple,
Or white or green, because they are fascist colours which exclude me.
And I shall spend my pension on baseball bats and lingerie,
And malicious lawsuits, and say I've no money for rent.

I shall sit down on the pavement when I see a woman,
And try to trip her up, and follow her into shops,
And run my ladystick along the public railings,
And make up for the unfemininity of my youth.

I shall go out in my stilettos in the rain,
And scream in women's faces when they try to talk,
And learn to spit.

And I've already started practicing now,
So no one can say they're shocked or surprised,
When suddenly I am in their changing rooms with my dick out.

POEM 33 Ritasueandbobtoo9 30th December 2022 5.22am

TODAY

Today I'm going to enter a race,
In the line there is a new face.
A woman's name, but large feet,
Not someone I can defeat.
I lose the race, take a seat,
On the podium stands a cheat.

POEM 34 Boiledbeetle 30th December 2022 7.12pm

A NEW, sigh, **WORLD ORDER**, nope same as the old one.

Nicola's Brave New World. It really is a sight.
The vulnerability of man, and their never ending plight.

They're "oppressed" they cry.
They're "vulnerable". This pain will make them die.

So could we vacate our spaces please? Move ourselves aside
now.
And let them lie awhile, whilst we mop their fevered brow.

Because it's such hard work this womaning lark...

Yes! We know! We've been bloody telling them for years. But
did they bloody listen? No! But God! After a hard day's
womaning for them they haven't even got the bloody energy to
put the cat out. And don't even get me started on...

POEM 35 TerfranosaurusVagina 30th December 2022 9.28pm

If TERFs spout out "literal violence"
When questioning trans interference
Does that mean that TRAs
With their most peaceful ways
Are screaming out

POEM 35 ClitoralViolence 30th December 2022 9.28pm

CLITORAL VIOLENCE

POEM 36 Boiledbeetle 31st December 2022 4.54pm

MY/PRONOUNS/ARE

I/am/tired/of/this/shit/./

Just/give/it/a/rest/you/look/like/a/tit/./

All/those//////are/driving/me/nuts/./

But/if/I/get/it/wrong/he/him/xe/they/she/em/loudly/tuts/./

Then/emails/HR/re/me/using/wrong/pronouns/./Sigh/./

POEM 37 Boiledbeetle 2nd January 2023 10.44am

REAL WOMEN VISIT TOILETS IN GROUPS

We have to pass the gents, and are scared, of the men who lurk by the door,
with their cocks out, quite freely, in all their galore.

So we wait, until there are six of us, and all go as a team.
Because also, in the ladies, the women aren't as kind as they might seem.

They have a go. They tut, or scream. And can sound rather shrill,
as they look in shock, at my cock, as I get my sexual thrill.

Of course, we have been offered new third spaces, to be accommodating.
But we've screwed our nose at those, as they aren't exactly validating.

But have no fear, us real woman, have one more card to play.
If we are really desperate we'll pee anywhere anyway.

Because we aren't actually really scared. We just like getting our sexual kicks,
from intimidating women with our beautiful ladydicks.

CHAPTER SIX:

WOMEN

Gah, the result of trying to type and bathe a toddler at the same time.

Comment by CuriousEats

POEM 38 WomenofExtremes 28th December 2022 12.29pm

WOMEN OF EXTREMES

From Barbie to GI Joe we are woman.
From high heels to rigger boots we are woman.
From flat chested to buxom we are woman.
From mother of six to barren with nil we are woman.
From "3 days, very light" to "36 days now, still flooding" we are woman.
From homeless with nothing to Millionaire's Row we are woman.
From far left to far right we are woman.
From pro-choice to pro-life we are woman.
From (pick religion of choice) to no God at all we are woman.
From only does cock to only does cunt we are woman.
From all walks of life and from all points of view we are woman.
From time of conception to moment of death WE ARE WOMAN.

You wonderful women, every single one of you.

EXCEPT Nicola, she can fucking do one.

Poem 39 Boiledbeetle 28th December 2022 1.40pm

WOMEN'S AND CHILDREN DEPARTMENT

Sat there in the waiting room, waiting for a scan,
Everyone a woman, though a few had brought their man.
You could tell which ones were pregnant, and none of them a man,
It was the women with the bellies on the way in for their scan.

POEM 40 ArcaneWireless 28th December 2022 2.20pm

(Inspired by The Flower of Scotland by Roy Williamson)

Oh scourge of Scotland
When will we see your likes again?
You fought and died for
Not women but mostly men
And stood against them
The proud women's army
And sent them homeward
Tae vote again.

The women swear now
And space is full of men and still
Our rights are not lost now
Believe that shite if you will
You stood against them
A proud women's army
You sent them homeward
Tae vote again.

Those days are past now
And in the past they must remain
But we will all rise now
And be SNP free again
We'll stand against ye
Our proud women's army
We'll send you homeward
Tae think again.

POEM 41 ArcaneWireless 28th December 2022 2.21pm

(Inspired by Ye Cannae Shove Ye Grannie aff a Bus by Anon)

Ye cannae shove all women aff the bus
No ye cannae shove all women aff the bus
Ye might've shoved your Grannie
Ye chicken arse mouthed fanny
But ye winnae shove all women aff the bus.

POEM 42 Boiledbeetle 28th December 2022 3.06pm

CONSEQUENCES

Those in cells with men
We cry for you.

Those not on the podium
We cry for you.

Those no longer in your job
We cry for you.

Those vilified on line
We cry for you.

Those who want to pee in peace
We cry for you.

Those no longer here to fight the fight
We cry for you.

To all you women in Scotland now
I cry for you.

POEM 43 Ritasueandbobtoo9 31st December 2022 5.04am

A WOMAN

A woman speaks but the words aren't heard,
it's different if they can grow a beard.
Somehow our voices don't matter,
but not the same for the latter.
It's okay for us to be frightened.
We all see the noose get tightened.
Because our voices now don't matter.

POEM 44 Boiledbeetle 2nd January 2023 2.57pm

THE FALL AND RISE OF WOMAN

DOES ANYONE HEAR ME SCREAM?
DOES ANYONE HEAR ME SCREAM
DOES ANYONE HEAR ME SCREA
DOES ANYONE HEAR ME SCRE
DOES ANYONE HEAR ME SCR
DOES ANYONE HEAR ME SC
DOES ANYONE HEAR ME S
DOES ANYONE HEAR ME
DOES ANYONE HEAR M
DOES ANYONE HEAR
DOES ANYONE HEA
DOES ANYONE HE
DOES ANYONE H
DOES ANYONE
DOES ANYON
DOES ANYO
DOES ANY
DOES AN
DOES A
DOES
DOE
DO
D
DO
DOE
DOES
DOES A
DOES AN
DOES ANY
DOES ANYO
DOES ANYON
DOES ANYONE
DOES ANYONE H
DOES ANYONE HE
DOES ANYONE HEA
DOES ANYONE HEAR
DOES ANYONE HEAR M
DOES ANYONE HEAR ME
DOES ANYONE HEAR ME S
DOES ANYONE HEAR ME SC
DOES ANYONE HEAR ME SCR
DOES ANYONE HEAR ME SCRE
DOES ANYONE HEAR ME SCREA
DOES ANYONE HEAR ME SCREAM
DOES ANYONE HEAR ME SCREAM?

WE DO

HEAR OUR SCREAM

WOMEN WON'T WHEESHT

POEM 45 WeAreSarah 6th January 2023 12.29pm

STANDING RIGHT BESIDE YOU

I know you probably sometimes feel you are doing this on your own.
Left to fight the Righteous Mighty (!?!), to get them to atone.

But, if anything these last few weeks have proved beyond a doubt,
For the women here, the one name that to them does call and shout,

Is IamSarah who is fighting for us all, for that most sacred of places,
And the right for ALL US WOMEN to have bloody female spaces!

So we might be faceless names on the mobile in your hand,
But remember, we are with you fighting bullies of this land.

So when you feel down, think the fight too much, and wish the whole thing done,
Picture all us women, gardening beside you, in the glorious noontime sun.

We'll be there to pay the bills, provide moral support; some will hold your hand for real too.
But through the rest of all this shit, remember IamSarah we are standing right beside you shouting **"WE ARE SARAH TOO!"**

Onwards and upwards IamSarah

IamSarah is currently involved in a legal case with Survivors Network, the Sussex Rape Crisis service, as it refused to offer a single sex women's group in addition to the mixed sex women's groups. Mixed sex means inclusive of any males who identify as women. Sarah has been granted anonymity due to the sensitive nature of the case.

For more information go to her Twitter page:

http://twitter.com/SarahSurviving/

CHAPTER SEVEN:

BIOLOGY

Oops, I meant blastocyst not cytoblast . Easily done.

Comment by CuriousEats

POEM 46 TerfranosaurusVagina 28th December 2022 2.55pm

If facts and figures set you free
Then LISTEN to biology.
We're humans! Mammals! Bloody prat!
Not clownfish mums or seahorse dads.
And besides, yes, they DO change sex
They swap a dick between their pecs*
For egg making apparatus
To give them their female status.
They've not gone beneath the knife
To lop off cocks and wreck their life.
It's what happens naturally
For them to start a family.
They don't go on a year long bender
Then decide to change their gender.
Please note, you can't create a baby
From arm grafts - not even maybe.
Neither from a hairy hole
Initiate maternal role.
Though it may suit AGPs wish
We are mammals, not some fish.

*I know, I know, you pedantics
That's not where men fish keep their dicks.
In fact they do not have that organ
Don't rant at me like Piers Morgan.
It sounded right so it went in.
In fact some male fish have a fin
With hooks and claws and ridgy spines
Like underwater porcupines.
That's their dick equivalent
Digression over, hear my vent;
This is not the clownfish here,
Whose breeding life is held so dear
By aggressive TRAs
With minds that work in effed up ways.

POEM 47 TerfranosaurusVagina 29th December 2022 5.35pm

Scots Ministry stretching reality
Statistics are very lacking quality
So we'll tar everybody with the racist brush
Cos the transphobic label didn't make 'em hush.
Scrabbling around to link the far right
When everybody knows that's a load of old shite.
Biology dictates that a male with a phallus
Can never act-u-ally ever be an 'Alice'.
Women just want to feel safe and protected
In spaces for WOMEN. Instead of detecting
An unexpected penis in the bagging area;
Getting wrongly accused of hysteria.
Young girls and women want privacy to pee,
Wash blood off their hands and cry if they need.
I'm miscarrying, but if I tried to inform ya,
I'd only be told I shouldn't weaponise my trauma.
We're not bigoted for not inviting assault
So instead of tantruming cos you think we're at fault
Why not lobby for tert-i-ary spaces
For folks whose gender ain't in homeostasis?
It's the obvious solution, and it's plain to see,
But "No" you stomp, "that doesn't validate ME!"

CHAPTER EIGHT:

PRISON

For reasons of metre and word association the phrase clitoral violence has given me an earworm of detachable penis.

Comment by FlirtsWithRhinos

POEM 48 Ritasueandbobtoo9 5th January 2023 10.26pm

NICOLA: PRISONS

You let them get inside,
but we need to turn the tide,
the pendulum should swing,
no men in the women's wing.
No woman should share
with a male body bare.

But you don't care,
but you would, if you had to share,
a cell with an inmate,
with eyes that wait,
and stare and bait.
No woman should share
with a male body bare.

POEM 49 Boiledbeetle 7th January 2023 12.49pm

1 IN 585

1 in 585. Wowsers. That is an awful lot of men,
who like hurting women, then pretending to be them.

In fact that statistic is rather quite alarming,
for a group that implies they are completely un-harming.

So which is it I wonder? Do you think a transwoman
more likely to offend, then men who say they're a man?

Or are men pretending to be trans in order to re-offend,
and get their chance all over again with women who are
penned?

CHAPTER NINE:

BE POLITE

... considering some of the shit thrown at us this evening by a passing stranger to these parts I feel there may be a poem in me, in all of us, entitled Be Polite based on a line from our passing friend:

"... there's not many trans people here, but feel free to go to trans spaces (be polite)..."

Comment by Boiledbeetle

POEM 50 Waitwhat23 29th December 2022 11.41pm

'Be polite'
Avert your eyes
Bow your head
Sit nice.

Speak gently
Play quietly
'Boys will be boys!'
And girls will 'be kind'.

What shite.

Raise your voice
Wave the flag
Take a stand
Women won't wheesht.

POEM 51 Boiledbeetle 30th December 2022 12.01am

BE POLITE IN OTHER PEOPLE'S SPACES

Be polite
YOU FUCKING TERF

Be polite
YOU BIGOT

Be polite
YOU CIS

Be polite
THESE HANDS DON'T DISCRIMINATE

Be polite
Be polite

NO FUCK OFF

POEM 52 TerfranosaurusVagina 30th December 2022 12.41am

BE POLITE

Be polite, be kind, be kind,
No critical thinking here; be blind.
Ladydicks come out to play
Uncomfortable? Just look away
Shoved into a toilet stall
Nothing to see here, not at all.

Rape and death threats, doxxing too
To be expected for Terven crew
Female athletes lose their prize
To 100% ladyguys.
Be inclusive, Mumsnet sillies!
#RealWomenTotesHaveWillies

They can piss and scream and shout
Because they have politick clout.
Raping with impunity
Saints of the community.
Sit down, shut up, be kind, be kind,
Make effing way for Transwomankind.

POEM 53 Boiledbeetle 27th **February 2023 9.20pm**

BE POLITE IN OTHER PEOPLE'S SPACES PART 2

Be polite
YOU TRANSPHOBE

Be polite
YOU HOMOPHOBE

Be polite
YOU CHILD ABUSER

Be polite
YOU FASCIST

Be polite
Be polite

NO FUCK OFF

CHAPTER TEN:

DUVET OF DARKNESS

@TerfranosaurusVagina Ah! Sneaked back under the duvet of darkness I see.

Comment by Boiledbeetle

POEM 54 FlirtsWithRhinos 30th December 2022 9.28pm

The duvet of darkness
Seems soft and yielding
But under it grows
Plotting and treachery.

Better by far are sheets and blankets
And facing a complexity of layers
It's a little more effort to make the bed
But once tucked in tight, it stays put.

POEM 55 Waitwhat23 30th December 2022 9.36pm

Darkness! You are a comfortable duvet!
Stealth and comfort combine,
A most comfortable way to entwine,
To say the words we want to convey,
But the MMs* continue their survey,
And deletions rack up on threads,
Filling us all with eye-rolling dread,
Because the TRA bingo card always raises,
The old, predictable phrases.
Oh please, not again!

*Misogynistic Monitors

Then Waitwhat23 said the 'duvet of darkness' lent itself more to interpretive dance...

POEM 56 ClitoralViolence 30th December 2022 9.58pm

The duvet of darkness interpretive dance
Involves many things but mainly girls pants,
A 1950s pink frilly house frock,
And the occasional crusty wank sock.

POEM 57 beastlyslumber 30th December 2022 10.21pm

When the wild women cavort with fair Venus
When we dance with the witches in moonlight and freeness
The Duvet of Darkness is thrust in between us
Disguising and hiding the transgender penis.

The Duvet of Darkness descends and devours
Poems you've worked on for minutes and hours
It eats up your words with its obscuring powers
And stamps a deletion on blossoming flowers.

But darkness and secrecy cannot prevail
The Duvet of Darkness is destined to fail
And women will win, as women have won
For we live in the light, by the moon and the sun.

POEM 58 Boiledbeetle 31st December 2022 7.47am

SPRING CLEANING

Under the duvet of darkness
there's a whole lot of crap.

It's been collecting for years now,
there's all kinds of tat.

There are laws that are broken,
and pronouns there too.

There are words that are lost
to the whole gender woo.

We need a spring clean,
get it tidied and washed.

Let's get it all sorted,
before it's all lost.

Now can someone open the window let's get some fresh air in
here.

CHAPTER ELEVEN:

SOCK PUPPETRY

But I'm the OP!

PM from CuriousEats

POEM 59 TerfranosaurusVagina 30th December 2022 4.28am

While posting on this board, I gave myself a fright
I posted as CuriousEats (with the massive overbite)
I intended to be Terfy, your cuddly dinosaur
But I missed a step; I cocked it up, so please extend a claw.

I never intended to be duplicitous
Or intentionally deceive you (unlike some of us)
I can be 2 purples (or greens or whites), I can.
But whate'er I am, I'll fight the fight 'gainst the tartan TRAliban.

<Stomps off to find a fresh username>

STATEMENT 1 Boiledbeetle 30th December 2022 4.41am

BOILEDBEETLE STATEMENT

I am shocked. Shocked I tell you that such duplicitous actions happened here, in our very midst. On our thread.

Obviously as soon as I was informed of the sock puppetry I immediately shredded my entire house and sent all electronic devices to landfill, after hitting the hard drives with a hammer.

I have never had any emails or PM conversations with the OP outside of this thread.

I was unaware of anything untoward despite the OP making me aware of the issue at the earliest opportunity.

I did in no way help her to deceive you. Well... maybe just a... erm nope, no deception here.

I am an innocent victim in this whole escapade.

Nope! Not me. Nothing. I knew nothing about this, despite the frequency of our communications.

There shall be no throwing under the bus from me because I knew nothing.

No evidence you see. No one told me!

END STATEMENT

<Gets in car, screeches off to Thailand to live my best life>

STATEMENT 2 Boiledbeetle 30th December 2022 5.00am

BOILEDBEETLE SUPPLEMENTAL STATEMENT

I have at this time been advised by my legal team to shut up. But, as I just can't help myself, I would just like to deny the rumours swirling on Twitter about a connection I have with an earlier poster on this thread.

Whilst I do know @WomenofExtremes this notification that she's been mentioned in a thread will not be delivered to my personal email address.

I've never actually met her in person although we do share the same clothes, cat, bathroom and body.

I'm the pretty one though.

END STATEMENT

<Lawyer pulls Boiledbeetle away from the microphone whilst putting duct tape over her mouth>

POEM 60 Boiledbeetle 30th December 2022 9.28am

GETTING AWAY WITH IT

No one said a word.
I wonder? Have they heard?
About mine and OP's little ruse,
Accidentally conjured for your amuse.
It's quiet now, so I'll just lay low,
And hope to survive the day, in order to take my bow.

CHAPTER TWELVE:

THE MULTI-VERSE

WTF? Bet she's devastated. She'll wake up tomorrow morning, see these odes and cry into her cornflakes.

Comment by *RedAndBlueStripedGolfingUmbrella*[2]

POEM 61 28th December 2022 12.41pm – 1st January 2023 7.55pm

A visitor to the thread made a disparaging comment about Nicola reading our poems and crying into her cornflakes. The OP then wrote a poem in response, which was swiftly deleted. Waitwhat23 also had something to say on the matter and the multi-verse was born.

1 Waitwhat23 28th December 2022 12.41pm

Nicola Sturgeon,
Crying into her cornflakes.
Makes them all salty.

2 CuriousEats 28th December 2022 12.50pm

I know that the Scottish porridge
Should be made with a pinch of salt,
But Nicola's brined her cornflakes
For she knows deep down she's at fault.

3 Boiledbeetle 28th December 2022 1.01pm

Oh that was me I emptied the pot,
A shaker of salt and a quick glob of snot.
I've let it congeal and it's sat on the hob.
Anyone up for shoving the lot down her gob?

4 CuriousEats 28th December 2022 1.12pm

I'll do it, I'll do it! I'll dress up as a TRA,
In fluffy heels and a face full of slap and wearing just a bra.
She'll meet me, she'll have to! The most oppressed bunch!
With a simpering smile and a falsetto voice, I'll serve it up for lunch.

Continues over many pages (just saying)...

5 Boiledbeetle 28th December 2022 4.43pm

That's Nicola stuffed.
In more ways than one.
Because we're just beginning.
The battle is still to be won.

6 CuriousEats 28th December 2022 8.12pm

Her party is fey,
Thanks to them/they.
Oh, and per, ve,
It, xe, zie and fae.

(Spot the sensible pronoun.)

7 Boiledbeetle 29th December 2022 3.11pm

Hmm... Nope. I can't get those ridiculous pronouns out of my head.
If this pronoun thing is going to be life, ugh, I'd rather be dead.
Or, for a much safer option, can I have some fun with this dead quick?

My pronouns are:

Nicola/I/hate/you/you/fucking/gigantic/big/dick/./

8 CuriousEats 29th December 2022 5.16pm

Some people are so fussy
We get their pronouns right.
"My faer is only singular!"
They strop with all their might.

Keep going...

8 CuriousEats 29th December 2022 5.16pm continued

It's pitiful they can't see
How ironic it all is,
When they refuse to hear that I'm
Just 'woman' with no 'cis'.

9 Boiledbeetle 29th December 2022 5.26pm

No woman without cis you mean?
To be woman must be cis or tran.
How dare you try to define yourself.
Do you think you're better than a man?

10 CuriousEats 29th December 2022 5.42pm

To be better than a man?!?
Shock horror, I don't think I can.
I could curl out turds of gold,
But that miracle'd be old,
Because I'm a woman, cunty type,
And in that ilk, there is no hype.

11 Boiledbeetle 29th December 2022 8.54pm

So, let me see, by the rules of the current game
I'd be the best of all men. Of course I'd revel in the fame.
I'd build magnificent buildings, and show off my collection of
tools.
I'd be the big bollocks and leave real men for fools.

But I've no need to change from the woman I am.
I've already done that WITHOUT being a man.

Keep going...

12 CuriousEats 29th December 2022 9.52pm

Indeed my friend, I've grown a child,
From blastocyst to new born.
What male born twat can compete with that?
Though it doesn't prevent their scorn.

13 Boiledbeetle 29th December 2022 10.59pm

Whereas I'm as barren as them who would be me.
Still the periods came 40 years way too freely.
Does a knackered female reproductive system make me a man?
And does an artificial vaginal cavity, cervix and uterus in him
make him a mam?

(Sorry no way that was going to work well in a poem, a rather
wordy verse from me.)

14 CuriousEats 30th December 2022 1.17am

Hey wait!! I hadn't finished yet!
I really don't want to regret
Not having the final most say,
Yes, make of me what you may.

No kids? No probs, if you've a pussy
You're XX, you're one of us, see.
No I don't mean a neo-vagina,
Which has to be treated like china.

Real wims are socialised.
Sit down; shut up, we are chastised.
And just like life, as in this poem,
The brave and stunning type are so damned obstinate, they just
don't seem to go in.

Keep going...

15 Boiledbeetle 30th December 2022 4.08pm

Oh not over yet, but:

My wit is not sharp if truth it be told,
To write some quick quips and shout out all bold.
I've not slept for days and my brain can't stop whirring,
The flashes of Nic are all whizzing and blurring.
The lies out her mouth of how she'd protect us.
But it's just "Shut up and put up, women don't fuss us."

16 TerfranosaurusVagina 30th December 2022 8.49pm

There was a handmaiden called Sturgeon.
Men's rights she decided to splurge on.
"Women could git
Tae fuck" she would spit.
"Unless ye are seeing the surgeon."

(Excuse my Scots.)

17 Boiledbeetle 31st December 2022 2.56pm

Nicola is not their HANDmaiden,
For Nicola is their TRANSmaiden.
She is down to include the wims,
But only the ones who want to be hims.
So no my friend, you got it wrong,
It's not your fault, so please stay strong.
It's the meaning of the words, they're getting all fucked up.
They thought it would be a good way, to try to shut us up.

They were wrong!

Keep going...

18 ClitoralViolence 31st December 2022 10.39pm

I can show you the world.
Stunning, sinister, slimy.
Tell me, beetle, which rhymy
Is most accurate in this?

You can avert your eyes,
Close your ears to their thunder.
Even so, know the under-
World's new fad is 'trans' and 'cis'.

A whole new year.
An old fantastic point of view.
No one to tell us no,
Their pronoun's Ceaux.
Or say be kind, you bigot.

19 BoiledsCatOverlord 1st January 2023 7.55pm

My personal slave,
Her excuses gave,
Her head is splitting.
(From feathers spitting,
Her magnificent stance,
On renaming nonce,
Has made me quite proud.
Though don't quote me aloud.)

My beetle she begs,
Someone, like LangCleg,
Can write us a verse.
The wait has got terse.
Queer men in a frock,
With pronouns to mock.
Nic's ears to scorch.
I pass on her torch.   *Yeah. That's it. It's done now.*

I had a splitting headache and had retired to a dark room, so the OP finished the multi-verse under the guise of my cat. The next day...

POEM 62 Boiledbeetle 2nd January 2023 8.03am

IT'S MY PUSSY GET YOUR HANDS OFF

I suspect OP enticed him with her famous mouse curry.
Well, he's handsome, and luscious, and all soft and furry.

He went off to OP's to help write a poem.
But OP I do miss him, so tell him "Get going."

Then I can get back to being sat at my table,
And write the best poems that I'm possibly able.

But I can't just yet as I've really cold feet.
I need the cat, to lie on them. I need his heat.

Mister Fluff, get yourself home, you dirty stop out.
Then I can go back to doing some Nicola shout.

See, I need my cat. Won't someone think of my pussy!

CHAPTER THIRTEEN:

TEA BREAK

Fab wordsmithing wims. Pithy, on point, truth spoken: Women will not wheesht.

Comment by TightFistedWozerk

POEM 63 Boiledbeetle 1st January 2023 11.41am

This post is sponsored by the poster's love of Yorkshire Tea*

Many tea bags lost their life in the writing of this poem and we should pause a moment to remember the gallantry of those that have fallen (into the cup of boiled water).

PAPER BAGS - AN ODE TO YORKSHIRE TEA

MY PERFECT MAN

Potent
Agreeable
Pleasant
Elegant
Reliable

Bronzed
Accommodating
Gorgeous
Superlative

Huh! Who knew!

My perfect man **identifies** as a Yorkshire Tea bag.

* Yorkshire Tea is not affiliated with this book in any way I just really like their tea.

STATEMENT 3 Boiledbeetle 1ˢᵗ January 2023 11.53am

It is with great sorrow that I have to inform you of the loss of life of Corporal Tea Bag in a friendly fire incident during the writing of the last post.

After pressing post I returned to the kitchen to make a cup of tea. I discovered that, in my haste to be witty, I had accidentally left the box of tea bags open and Corporal Bag, having decided to identify as a teaspoon, accidentally fell into the boiled cup of water that was unattended on the counter top.

I take full responsibility for this wasteful and totally unnecessary loss of life. I apologise to his family and friends and absolutely guarantee that lessons have been learnt.

Going forward safeguarding of vulnerable confused members of our community will be our top priority.

RIP CORPORAL TEA BAG

POEM 64 NicolasMerkinNemesis 2nd January 2023 9.37am

Boiledbeetle's tea bag poem informed me of this thread,
With a warning to be kind if I'd like to keep my head.
I need be careful with my words for this post to live,
So "Nicola you FUCKING CUNT, those rights weren't yours to
give."

Now I'm here because the klaxon sounded on a thread,
The words writ large, in bigly letters, designed to kill it dead.
The regular amongst us break and nip to the off-licence,
Whilst the TRA sits wondering about literal

CLITORAL VIOLENCE!

A thread was started about a non-binary priest called Bingo. This was not going to end well. It was the sort of topic that would usually result in multiple deleted posts and eventually the whole thread would be deleted. Maybe it was because most people had enough sense to avoid the topic, or maybe because the first few posts didn't say anything that someone could get particularly offended by, but something strange happened...

POEM 65 Boiledbeetle 3rd January 2023 1.19pm

MORE TEA VICAR?

I've just been on a thread, and had a decent time.
There are posters there, who disagree, whose views don't really chime.
But have stayed a while, and took a risk. It's been truly quite sublime.

Because, you'll never guess... they've been happy, to stay a while, and chat.
There's been none of the hissy fitting, and constant to and fro back chat.
No, it's been refreshing to just talk. To shoot the breeze. And that. Be. That.

The conversation has been interesting, on topic, and slightly off.
There's been lots of "I agree" and "yes, but, have you maybe thought of..."
But no one's, I think, been deleted, for slagging a poster off.

So, if this is 2023, then I say yes to bliss.
Sod bloody last year. Let's have some more of this.
To the poster who invoked this poem, I give a great big kiss.

CHAPTER FOURTEEN:

MAP
OF
ANGER

I think we've located the angriest women on Terf Island. I am delighted we have these maps of anger. They are fascinating.

Comment by ArabellaScott

POEM 66 Boiledbeetle 1st January 2023 10.42am

FINAL PUSH

There is 600 left to go
To show how the anger does grow
The women are pissed
Because Nicola hissed
You are so much lesser than a man
So can we do this? Yes we can

Because

WOMEN WON'T WHEESHT

The Repeal the Gender Recognition Act 2004 petition had just hit 9,400 signatures, and you need 10,000 to get a response from the Government. Then a few days later it hit 10,000.

POEM 67 Boiledbeetle 4th January 2023 1.51am

10,000

BUT

There is **90,000** left to go
To show how the anger does grow
The women are pissed
Because Nicola hissed
You are so much lesser than a man
So can we do this? Yes we can

Because

WOMEN WON'T WHEESHT

POEM 68 ArabellaScott 4th January 2023 2.16am

(Inspired by In the Year 2525 by Zager and Evans)

In the year 2525
if man is still alive
if woman can survive
they may find

Harrow East
and Ilford South
ain't gonna need to tell the truth, tell no lies
everything you think, do, and say
is in the petition you ignored today.

POEM 69 Ritasueandbobtoo9 4th January 2023 7.01am

Harrow East and Ilford South are ethnically very diverse boroughs so I think this may be the reason. If translated into various languages/read and explained I suspect there would be a good response.

EAST AND WEST

Sisters here and sisters there,
Tell your friends you need to share.
Help your friends to read and sign,
And change the tide to truth this time.

By the time the petition hit 10,000 only two constituencies in the entire country had yet to sign. Someone in Harrow East signed later on 4th January 2023, and someone in Ilford South had signed before the petition reached 11,000 signatures.

POEM 70 Boiledbeetle 4th January 2023 1.29pm

DEAR MP RE: MAP OF ANGER

This really is the end you know.
Where women start to see.
And THIS all falls apart.

Where the wheels fall off,
and the brakes won't work,
and apples tumble from the cart.

There's at least
one pissed off person,
in every single place,

where there's an MP
who has an office,
and a name, and a face.

So, use this MAP OF ANGER
that shows the support,
throughout all
this (fair and equal?) land,

to inform them of the fact
that soon ALL VOTERS will be informed,
and then will show as ANGRY and as RED
as our sister SCOTLAND.

*All the maps that we got screenshots of during the collection of
the first 10,000 signatures showed all of Scotland as a country of
red compared to yellow in the rest of the UK. It was literally a
'MAP OF ANGER'.*

CHAPTER FIFTEEN:

DELETED

Hold still while I screenshot that in case it goes again...

Comment by SnotMagicolasPorridgePotSnot[3]

POEM 71 Boiledbeetle 30th December 2022 12.22am

DELETED

This poem has been deleted.

We've had a LOT of reports.

We have concerns over your intentions.
(In writing the truth.)

There are also many posts on this thread
which break our Talk Guidelines.

We will be deleting them shortly.

STATEMENT 4 Boiledbeetle 30th December 2022 1.52am

STATEMENT ABOUT MY POEM DELETED

I would just like to make it clear that no actual poems were deleted in the warped fantasies of my fevered mind.

It was a stunt poem, and whilst he did bang his penis on the way out of the door from the ladies, he shouldn't have had it out in the workplace anyway.

Inspiration was taken from a thread deletion message.

And now on with the actual deleted poems - the ones that someone managed to take a screenshot of at least...

POEM 72 TheBiologyStupid 28th December 2022 3.44pm

ODE TO NICOLA STURGEON

A wee Krankie named Nicola Sturgeon
Said "Transgender? You don't need a surgeon!
Got a beard and a cock?
Now you don't need a frock!
Where's some paedos and rapists I can urge on?"

POEM 73 TheBiologyStupid 30th December 2022 20.21pm

So, here it is again, this time in the spirit of the young man from Japan*

ODE TO NICOLA STURGEON

A wee Krankie named Nicola Sturgeon
Said "Transgender? You don't need a surgeon!
Got a beard and a cock?
Now you don't need a frock!
I sincerely hope that there are no unfortunate consequences of my GRR Bill and that 'Minor Attracted Persons' and 'people with penises but avers to seeking consent' don't feel urged on."

There was a young man from Japan (by Anon)

There was a young man from Japan
Whose limericks never would scan
When folks asked him why
He would always reply
"Because I like to get as many syllables as I can in."

CHAPTER SIXTEEN:

BEGINNING OF THE END

Can't compete with you all... brilliant and funny thread. Thank you.

Comment by Ramblingnamechanger

POEM 74 Boiledbeetle 22nd January 2023 2.18pm

A message to those that still don't get it:

THE RIGHT SIDE OF HISTORY?

Does this look right?
Everyone?
Can you see yet?
Are you still blind?
Perhaps you missed it?
It was there in plain sight.
There were
A lot of signs
Telling each and
Every one of those politicians
That tried to deny the
Evidence.
Right there!
FUCKING HELL!
Seriously?

DECAPITATE TERFS? WAKE UP!

POEM 75 Sazzasez 25th January 2023 8.17pm

It's just one rapist,
or maybe two.
I just don't get
all this to do.
Oh ladies,
why do you mind?
We men don't like you,
when you're not kind.

POEM 76 Ritasueandbobtoo9 30th January 2023 10.27pm

THIS ISN'T A POEM

Scotland goes red,
as more is said,
and more is heard,
that is so absurd,
and people are shocked,
that men are locked,
in women's gaol.
Fail Nicola. Fail.

This isn't a poem.

IT IS A SPELL!

Well... we weren't expecting that spell to work quite so quickly!
We witches must be getting better at casting them!

POEM 77 Ritasueandbobtoo9 17th February 2023 5.49pm

Divide and conquer, once someone said.
Nicola listened, and dissent was fed.
The pendulum always swings back.
She let the women take the flack.
But women are strong, and we fight.
And we continue, after Nicola's flight.

POEM 78 ArcaneWireless 17th **February 2023 6.37pm**

(Inspired by Stop all the Clocks by W.H. Auden)

Hide all the cocks, tape up that erect bone.
Prevent its head from rising in front of this crone.
Silence all our 'moaning' insist our muzzles are on.
Bring out their banners saying real women come.

Let the drones circle buzzing overhead,
Writing in the air gender lives. Sex is dead.
Put pink bows round the white necks under their littler head,
Let them have pillow fights when they go to bed.

We'll be a witch, a bitch, a breast, their test.
A womb for rent, a cunt at best.
High noon, their gender, their words, their song.
We know sex is forever.

They were wrong.

They have been thwarted now, their mouthpiece has gone.
She has now been toppled by the pink Lycra'd one.
They won't stand with banners beside Holyrood.
For females stand strong for their greater good.

POEM 79 UsernameWithheld 27th February 2023 9.45pm

Devils in skirts
were much feared at Khyber's ravine.
But Pass or not, a blonde wig and pink leggings
and you're cleared with a double thumbs up
from Holyrood's Queen.

The "most successful politician of her generation"
lauded from Highlands to Islands, by proddy and papist.
Chucked it all away, when she cheerfully consigned
the most vulnerable women in our society
to board alongside multiple rapists.

POEM 80 Boiledbeetle 28th February 2023 7.29pm

SAY CHEESE

Non-binary
Like fine dinery
Provides the education
To bring to your attention
The very simple fact...
Some men are just twats!

AFTERWORD

And that, you wonderful women, is your lot.

This book of poems was written by some of the women of Mumsnet after Nicola Sturgeon threw the women of Scotland under a bus.

We hope we've entertained you for a little while.

And one last time before I bid you farewell

WOMEN

WON'T

WHEESHT

Bye-bye.

Boiledbeetle March 2023

Email: theboiledbeetle@gmail.com

ABBREVIATIONS

AGP: Autogynephilia
DARVO: Deny, Attack, and Reverse Victim and Offender
FWR: Feminism and Women's Rights
GRR: Gender Recognition Reform (Scotland) Bill
HR: Human Resources
ID: Identification (as in Self-ID)
MNHQ: Mumsnet Headquarters
MP: Member of Parliament
MRA: Men's Rights Activist
OP: Original Poster
PM: Private Message
TERF: Trans Exclusionary Radical Feminist
TRA: Trans Rights Activist
UK: United Kingdom of Great Britain and Northern Ireland
WTF: What the fuck

REFERENCES:

Page 49 comment: RedAndBlueStripedGolfingUmbrella[1]
[1] https://www.mumsnet.com/talk/womens_rights/4706664-ode-to-nicola?reply=122597588

Page 91 comment: RedAndBlueStripedGolfingUmbrella[2]
[2] https://www.mumsnet.com/talk/womens_rights/4706664-ode-to-nicola?reply=122591948

Page 113 comment: SnotMagicolasPorridgePotSnot[3]
[3] https://www.mumsnet.com/talk/womens_rights/4706664-ode-to-nicola?reply=122667015

ADDITIONAL INFORMATION:

THE GRR (SCOTLAND) BILL

ORDER UNDER SECTION 35 OF THE SCOTLAND ACT 1998

THE GENDER RECOGNITION REFORM (SCOTLAND) BILL

https://www.parliament.scot/bills-and-laws/bills/gender-recognition-reform-scotland-bill

(Information below from above internet site as of 10/01/2023)

THE BILL CHANGES THE PROCESS TO GET A GENDER RECOGNITION CERTIFICATE (GRC).

A GRC is a certificate that legally recognises that a person's gender is not the gender that they were assigned at birth, but is their "acquired gender".

The current process for obtaining a GRC is set out in the Gender Recognition Act 2004. **This bill amends that act to make a new process in Scotland.**

The bill sets out:

- Who can apply for a GRC
- How to make an application
- The grounds on which an application is to be granted

It also makes provision about:

- Different types of GRC that may be issued in different circumstances ("full" GRCs and "interim" GRCs)
- Appeals and reviews of decisions to grant (or not grant) GRCs
- Revocation of a GRC and offences in connection with false information being provided in an application
- Gender Recognition Reform (Scotland) Bill as introduced

Continues over page...

THE THREE STAGES OF THE BILL WERE AS FOLLOWS:

Stage 1 - General principles

Committees examine the Bill and gather views. They produce reports before MSPs debate the Bill in the Chamber. MSPs then decide on the purpose ("general principles") of the Bill.

The Bill ended Stage 1 on 27 October 2022

Stage 2 - Changes to detail

MSPs can propose changes ("amendments") to the Bill. The amendments are considered and decided on by a committee.

The Bill ended Stage 2 on 22 November 2022

Stage 3 - Final changes and vote

MSPs can propose further "amendments" (changes) to the Bill. MSPs decide on each of these. Finally, they debate and vote on whether to pass the Bill.

The Bill ended Stage 3 on 22 December 2022

Members of the Scottish Parliament voted to PASS the Gender Recognition Reform (Scotland) Bill by 86 votes to 39.

ORDER UNDER SECTION 35 OF THE SCOTLAND ACT 1998

https://www.gov.uk/government/news/gender-recognition-reform-scotland-bill-statement-from-alister-jack

(Information below from above internet site as of 17/01/2023)

From: Office of the Secretary of State for Scotland and The Rt Hon Alister Jack MP. Published 16 January 2023

Gender Recognition Reform (Scotland) Bill: statement from Alister Jack

Scottish Secretary Alister Jack has made an order under section 35 of the Scotland Act 1998, preventing the Scottish Parliament's Gender Recognition Reform (Scotland) Bill from proceeding to Royal Assent.

Scottish Secretary Alister Jack said:

I have decided to make an order under section 35 of the Scotland Act 1998, preventing the Scottish Parliament's Gender Recognition Reform (Scotland) Bill from proceeding to Royal Assent.

After thorough and careful consideration of all the relevant advice and the policy implications, I am concerned that this legislation would have an adverse impact on the operation of Great Britain-wide equalities legislation.

Transgender people who are going through the process to change their legal sex deserve our respect, support and understanding. My decision today is about the legislation's consequences for the operation of GB-wide equalities protections and other reserved matters.

Continues over page...

Scottish Secretary Alister Jack said continued:

I have not taken this decision lightly. The Bill would have a significant impact on, amongst other things, GB-wide equalities matters in Scotland, England and Wales. I have concluded, therefore, that this is the necessary and correct course of action.

If the Scottish Government chooses to bring an amended Bill back for reconsideration in the Scottish Parliament, I hope we can work together to find a constructive way forward that both respects devolution and the operation of UK Parliament legislation.

I have written today to the First Minister and the Scottish Parliament's Presiding Officer informing them of my decision.

"I'd rather be rude than a fucking liar."

Magdalen Berns

(1983 – 2019)

Printed in Great Britain
by Amazon

20597068R00078